Especially for

_____

From

_____

Date

_____

Compiled by Kathy Shutt.

ISBN 978-1-61626-317-1

Published by Barbour Publishing, Inc., P.O. Box 719, Uhrichsville, Ohio 44683, www.barbourbooks.com

Our mission is to publish and distribute inspirational products offering exceptional value and biblical encouragement to the masses.

Member of the
Evangelical Christian
Publishers Association

Printed in China.

Words to Live By. . .
for Moms

BARBOUR
PUBLISHING

Maternal love!
Thou word that sums all bliss.

ROBERT POLLOCK

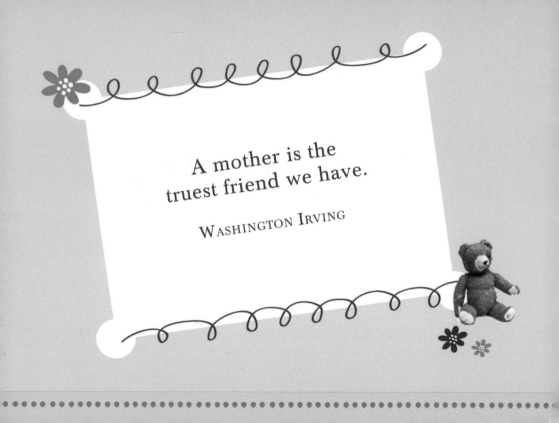

A mother is the
truest friend we have.

WASHINGTON IRVING

Motherhood:
All love begins and ends there.

ROBERT BROWNING

A mother's heart is always with her children.

PROVERB

A mother's happiness is like a beacon, lighting up the future but reflected also on the past in the guise of fond memories.

HONORÉ DE BALZAC

Why did God make mothers?
To teach us how to love Him.
To teach us how to love.

LARISSA CARRICK

No language can express the power and beauty and heroism of a mother's love.

EDWIN CHAPIN

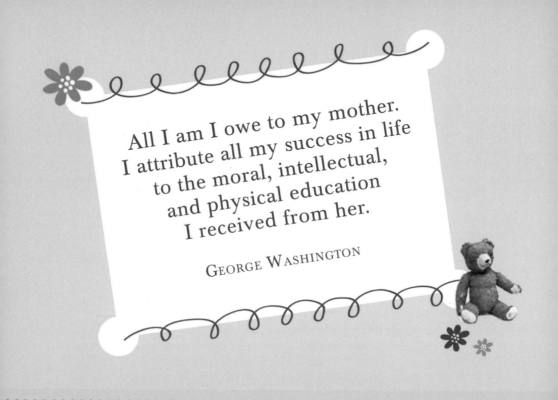

All I am I owe to my mother.
I attribute all my success in life
to the moral, intellectual,
and physical education
I received from her.

GEORGE WASHINGTON

*A mother's love perceives
no impossibilities.*

PADDOCK

Meet God in the morning and
go with Him through the day,
And thank Him for His guidance
each evening when you pray.

HELEN STEINER RICE

*Blessed be your discretion
and advice, and blessed be you.*

1 Samuel 25:33 amp

As in the Master's spirit you take into your arms the little ones. His own everlasting arms will encircle them and you. He will pity both their and your simplicity; and as in unseen presence He comes again, His blessing will breathe upon you.

James Hamilton

Bitter are the tears of a child: Sweeten them.
Deep are the thoughts of a child: Quiet them.
Sharp is the grief of a child: Take it from him.
Soft is the heart of a child: Do not harden it.

PAMELA GLENCONNER

I never knew how much love
my heart could hold until
someone called me "Mommy."

UNKNOWN

*People are what
their mothers make them.*

RALPH WALDO EMERSON

Youth fades; love droops;
the leaves of friendship fall;
A mother's secret hope outlives them all.

OLIVER WENDELL HOLMES

*You know you're a mom
when you say things like. . .
"You're not leaving the house
dressed like that."*

VICKIE PHELPS

The three most beautiful sights:
a potato garden in bloom, a ship in sail,
a woman after the birth of her child.

IRISH PROVERB

*Mother is the bank where we deposit
all our hurts and worries.*

UNKNOWN

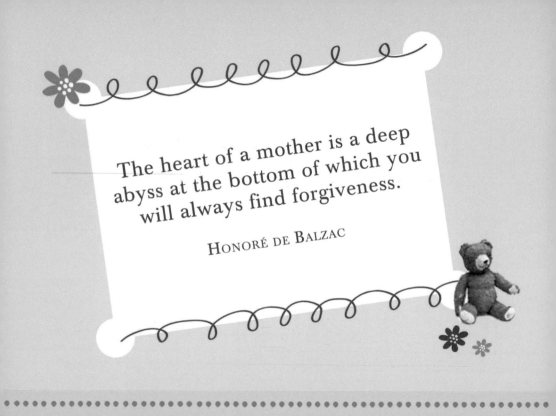

The heart of a mother is a deep abyss at the bottom of which you will always find forgiveness.

HONORÉ DE BALZAC

A mother is the one who is still there when everyone else has deserted you.

UNKNOWN

There is in every true woman's heart a spark of heavenly fire, which lies dormant in the broad daylight of prosperity, but which kindles up and beams and blazes in the dark hour of adversity.

WASHINGTON IRVING

The woman who creates and
sustains a home, and under
whose hands children
grow up to be strong
and pure men and women,
is a creator second only to God.

HELEN HUNT JACKSON

You will find as you look back upon your life that the moments when you have truly lived are the moments when you have done things in the spirit of love.

HENRY DRUMMOND

Be the living expression of God's kindness:
kindness in your face, kindness in your eyes,
kindness in your smile.

MOTHER TERESA

A gentle answer turns away wrath, but a harsh word stirs up anger.

PROVERBS 15:1 NASB

Home is where the heart can bloom.

CHARLES SWAIN

Listen to your mother's stories; know her history.

VICKIE PHELPS

A mother is a person who seeing there are only four pieces of pie for five people, promptly announces she never did care for pie.

TENNEVA JORDAN

Always laugh when you can.
It is cheap medicine.

LORD BYRON

*A mother understands
what a child does not say.*

JEWISH PROVERB

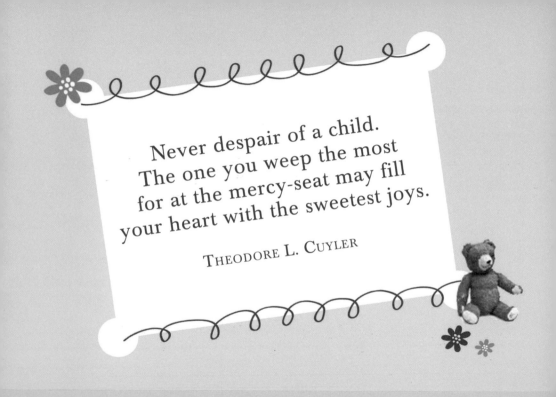

Never despair of a child.
The one you weep the most
for at the mercy-seat may fill
your heart with the sweetest joys.

THEODORE L. CUYLER

God has given you your child,
that the sight of him, from time to time,
might remind you of His goodness,
and induce you to praise Him
with filial reverence.

CHRISTIAN SCRIVER

Mothers hold their children's hands for a short while, but their hearts forever.

UNKNOWN

Live neither in the past nor in the future, but let each day's work absorb your entire energies and satisfy your widest ambition.

Sir William Osler

The thing about daughters is. . .they need the love
the most when they are hardest to love.

ELLYN SANNA

Love isn't how you feel.
It's what you do.

MADELEINE L'ENGLE

Every mother is like Moses;
she does not enter
the Promised Land.
She prepares a world
she will not see.

POPE PAUL VI

*Making a decision to have
a child—it's momentous.
It is to decide forever to have
your heart go walking around
outside your body.*

ELIZABETH STONE

Think of the sacrifice
your mother had to make
in order that you might live.
Think of the sacrifice God
had to make that you and
your mother might live.

UNKNOWN

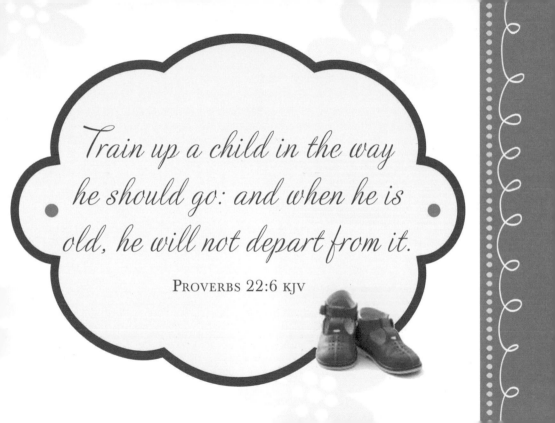

Train up a child in the way he should go: and when he is old, he will not depart from it.

PROVERBS 22:6 KJV

No one in the world can take the place of your mother. Right or wrong, from her viewpoint you are always right.

HARRY TRUMAN

Women know. . .a simple, merry knack of
tying sashes, fitting baby shoes, and stringing
pretty words that make no sense.

ELIZABETH BARRETT BROWNING

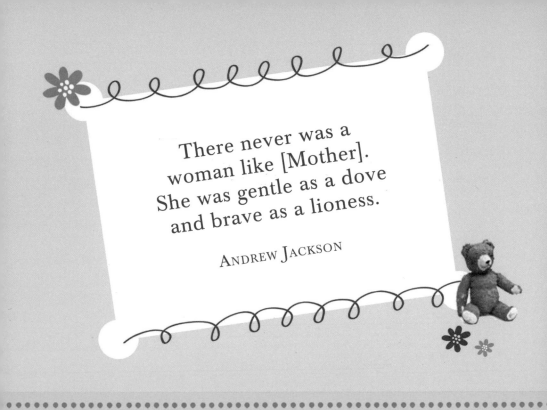

There never was a
woman like [Mother].
She was gentle as a dove
and brave as a lioness.

ANDREW JACKSON

My mother had a slender, small body, but a large heart—a heart so large that everybody's joys found welcome in it, and hospitable accommodation.

MARK TWAIN

My sainted mother taught
me a devotion to God
and a love to country
which have ever sustained
me in my many lonely and
bitter moments of decision in
distant and hostile lands.
To her, I yield anew a
son's reverent devotion.

General Douglas MacArthur

Becoming a mother makes you the mother of all children. You long to comfort all who are desolate.

CHARLOTTE GRAY

*A mother is not a person to lean on,
but a person to make leaning unnecessary.*

DOROTHY CANFIELD FISHER

A good mother is worth
a hundred schoolmasters.

GEORGE HERBERT

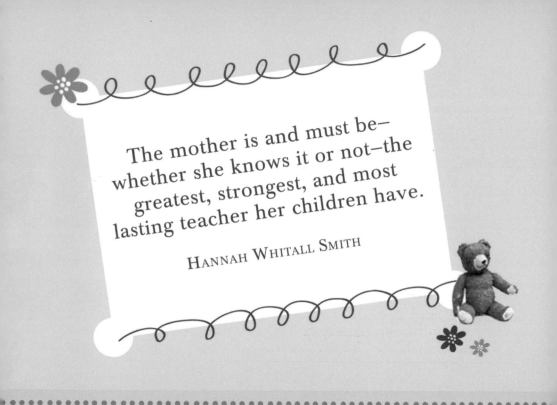

The mother is and must be—
whether she knows it or not—the
greatest, strongest, and most
lasting teacher her children have.

HANNAH WHITALL SMITH

Maternal love:
A miraculous substance
which God multiplies as He divides it.

VICTOR HUGO

Family: Those who know
you as you really are,
understand where you've been,
accept who you've become,
and still gently invite
you to grow.

ABRAHAM LINCOLN

Mother love is the fuel that enables a normal human being to do the impossible.

MARION C. GARRETTY

I love my mother as the trees love
water and sunshine—she helps me grow, prosper,
and reach great heights.

ADABELLA RADICI

A mother's arms are made of tenderness,
and children sleep soundly in them.

VICTOR HUGO

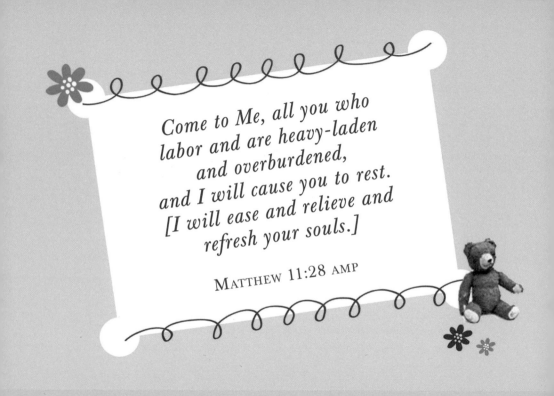

Come to Me, all you who
labor and are heavy-laden
and overburdened,
and I will cause you to rest.
[I will ease and relieve and
refresh your souls.]

MATTHEW 11:28 AMP

Education commences at the mother's knee, and every word spoken within hearsay of little children tends toward the formation of character.

HOSEA BALLOU

My mom is a never-ending song in my heart of comfort, happiness, and being. I may sometimes forget the words, but I always remember the tune.

GRAYCIE HARMON

Do not spoil what you have
by desiring what you have not;
but remember that what you
now have was once among
the things you only hoped for.

EPICURUS

Very little is needed to make a happy life.

MARCUS AURELIUS ANTONIUS

I am still determined to be cheerful and happy in whatever situation I may be, for I have also learned from experience that the greater part of our happiness or misery depends on our dispositions and not on our circumstances.

MARTHA WASHINGTON

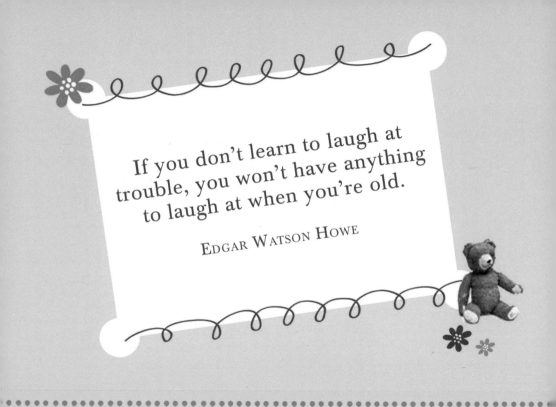

If you don't learn to laugh at trouble, you won't have anything to laugh at when you're old.

EDGAR WATSON HOWE

A child is a beam of sunlight from the Infinite and Eternal, with possibilities of virtue and vice— but as yet unstained.

LYMAN ABBOT

*Children have more need
of models than
of critics.*

JOSEPH JOUBERT

He who every morning plans the transaction of the day and follows out that plan, carries a thread that will guide him through the maze of the most busy life.
But where no plan is laid. . .
chaos will soon reign.

VICTOR HUGO

Education is the mental railway, beginning at birth and running on to eternity. No hand can lay it in the right direction but the hand of a mother.

Mrs. H. O. Ward

Get happiness out of your work,
or you may never know what happiness is.

ELBERT HUBBARD

Measure not the work
until the day's out
and the labor done.

ELIZABETH BARRETT BROWNING

The real religion of this world
comes from women much more
than from men—from mothers most of all,
who carry the key of our souls in their bosoms.

Oliver Wendell Holmes

A life filled with love
must have some thorns;
but a life empty of love
will have no roses.

UNKNOWN

*Who can find
a virtuous woman?
for her price is far
above rubies.*

PROVERBS 31:10 KJV

When God thought of mother,
He must have laughed with satisfaction,
and framed it quickly—so rich, so deep,
so divine, so full of soul, power,
and beauty, was the conception.

HENRY WARD BEECHER

*Mothers are the most
instinctive philosophers.*

HARRIET BEECHER STOWE

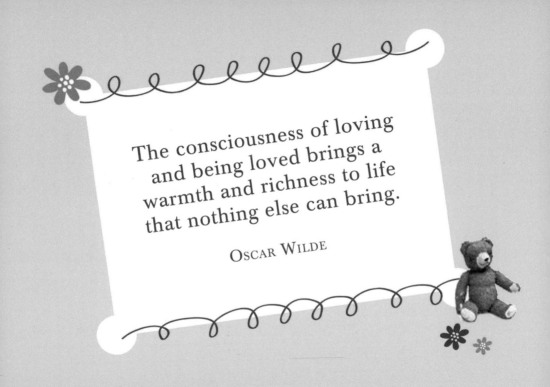

The consciousness of loving
and being loved brings a
warmth and richness to life
that nothing else can bring.

OSCAR WILDE

Home is where one starts from.

T. S. ELIOT

The successful mother,
the mother who does her part
in rearing and training aright
the boys and girls who are to be
the men and women of the next
generation, is of greater use
to the community. . . .
She is more important
by far than the successful
statesman or businessman
or artist or scientist.

THEODORE ROOSEVELT

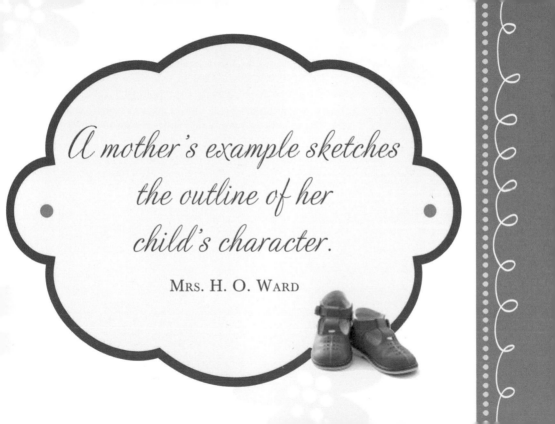

A mother's example sketches the outline of her child's character.

MRS. H. O. WARD

No man is poor
who has a godly mother.

ABRAHAM LINCOLN

Thank You, God, for pretending
not to notice that one of Your angels is
missing and for guiding her to me.
Sometimes I wonder what special
name You had for her.
I call her "Mother."

BERNICE MADDUX

A mother. . .fills a place so great that there isn't an angel in heaven who wouldn't be glad to give a bushel of diamonds to come down here and take her place.

BILLY SUNDAY

Through the ages no nation has had a better friend than the mother who taught her child to pray.

UNKNOWN

Real joy comes not from
ease or riches or from
the praise of men,
but from doing something
worthwhile.

Sir Wilfred Grenfell

We worry about what a child will become tomorrow; yet we forget that he is someone today.

STACIA TAUSCHER

What God is to the world,
parents are to their children.

PHILO

God could not be everywhere,
and therefore He made mothers.

RUDYARD KIPLING

The older women. . .can urge the younger women to love their husbands and children, to be self-controlled and pure, to be busy at home, to be kind.

TITUS 2:3–5 NIV

Mothers are like fine collectibles —
as the years go by,
they increase with value.

UNKNOWN

*Motherhood is priced
of God, at price no man
may dare to lessen
or misunderstand.*

HELEN HUNT JACKSON

You may have tangible
wealth untold;
caskets of jewels and
coffers of gold.
Richer than I you can never be,
I had a mother who read to me.

STRICKLAND GILLIAN

The tie which links a mother and child
is of such pure and immaculate strength
as to never be violated.

WASHINGTON IRVING

Children and mothers never truly part,
Bound in the beating of each other's heart.

CHARLOTTE GRAY

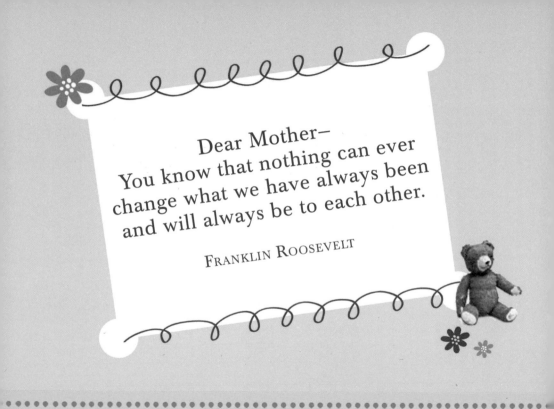

Dear Mother—
You know that nothing can ever
change what we have always been
and will always be to each other.

FRANKLIN ROOSEVELT

The mother love is like God's love;
He loves us not because we are lovable,
but because it is His nature to love,
and because we are His children.

EARL RINEY

Happy the son whose faith in his mother remains unchanged.

LOUISA MAY ALCOTT

"Isn't there one child you really love the best?" a mother was asked. And she replied, "Yes. The one who is sick, until he gets well; the one who's away, until he gets home."

UNKNOWN

The hand that rocks the cradle rules the world.

WILLIAM ROSS WALLACE

Many of us have inherited great riches
from our parents—the bank account
of their personal faith and family prayers.

NELS F. S. FERRE

A mother's children are portraits of herself.

UNKNOWN

Though we lay down our lives for her,
we can never pay the debt we owe
to a Christian mother.

UNKNOWN

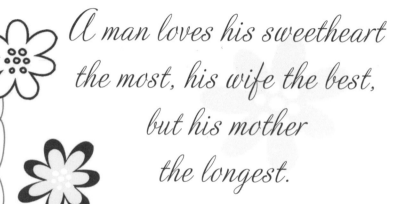

A man loves his sweetheart the most, his wife the best, but his mother the longest.

IRISH PROVERB

*Children are a gift
from the Lord;
they are a reward from him.*

PSALM 127:3 NLT

Even He who died for us upon the cross was mindful of His mother, as if to teach us that this holy love should be our last worldly thought.

Henry Wadsworth Longfellow

God pardons like a mother who kisses the offense into everlasting forgetfulness.

HENRY WARD BEECHER

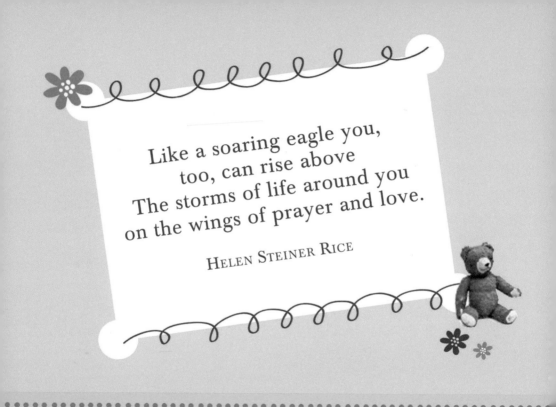

Like a soaring eagle you,
too, can rise above
The storms of life around you
on the wings of prayer and love.

HELEN STEINER RICE

The mother is everything—
she is our consolation in sorrow,
our hope in misery,
and our strength in weakness.

KAHLIL GIBRAN

Once we were simply
mother and child.
That hasn't changed,
but now we have
become even more.
Now we are friends.

ELLYN SANNA

Let the ways of childish confidence and freedom from care. . .teach you what should be your ways with God.

HANNAH WHITALL SMITH

Dreams are the touchstone of our character.

HENRY DAVID THOREAU

If peace be in the heart,
the wildest winter storm
is full of solemn beauty.

C. F. RICHARDSON

*The love of God
accomplishes all things
quietly and completely.*

LILIAN WHITING

*Set your thoughts not on the storm,
but on the Love that rules the storm.*

MRS. CHARLES E. COWMAN

The thing about mothers is. . .they are—each and every one—the best cooks in the entire world.

ELLYN SANNA

*Let a nation
have good mothers
and she will have good sons.*

NAPOLEON BONAPARTE

We are shaped and
fashioned by what we love.

JOHANN WOLFGANG VON GOETHE

No act of kindness,
no matter how small, is ever wasted.

AESOP

*My voice shalt thou
hear in the morning,
O LORD; in the morning will
I direct my prayer unto thee,
and will look up.*

PSALM 5:3 KJV

Who takes a child by the hand takes the mother by the heart.

DANISH PROVERB

*Children are what
the mothers are.
No father's fondest
care can fashion
so the infant heart.*

W. S. LANDOR

*Children are the anchors
that hold a mother to life.*

SOPHOCLES

I never understood the obstacles
my mother faced until I became one.
I love my mother's memory now more than ever.

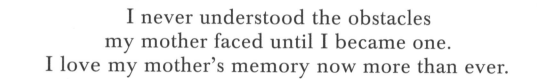

UNKNOWN

*The best gift a mother can give
her child is the gift of herself.*

UNKNOWN

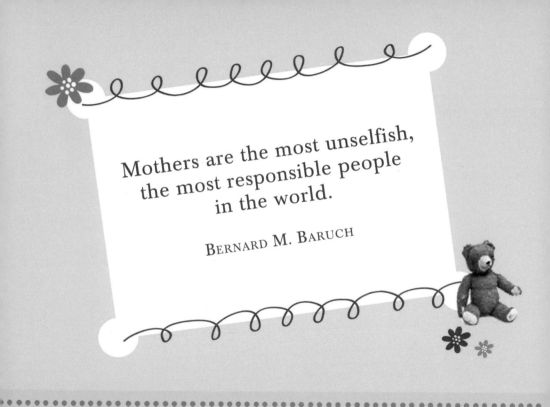

Mothers are the most unselfish,
the most responsible people
in the world.

BERNARD M. BARUCH

*It was when I had my first child
that I understood how much
my mother loved me.*

UNKNOWN

The mother's heart is the child's schoolroom.

HENRY WARD BEECHER

Rejecting things because
they are old-fashioned would rule
out the sun and the moon—
and a mother's love.

UNKNOWN

There are only two lasting
bequests we can hope to give our children.
One is roots; and the other, wings.

HODDING CARTER

It is in the everyday and commonplace that we learn patience, acceptance, and contentment.

RICHARD J. FOSTER

Go to sleep in peace.
God is awake.

VICTOR HUGO

Everything we call a trial,
a sorrow, or duty, believe me,
that an angel's hand is there.

FRA GIOVANNI

A joyful and pleasant thing it is to be thankful.

BOOK OF COMMON PRAYER

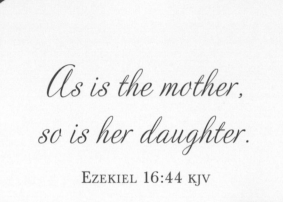

As is the mother,
so is her daughter.

EZEKIEL 16:44 KJV

Holy as heaven a mother's tender love,
The love of many prayers and many tears which
changes not with dim, declining years.

CAROLINE NORTON

Babies are always more trouble than you thought—and more wonderful.

CHARLES OSGOOD

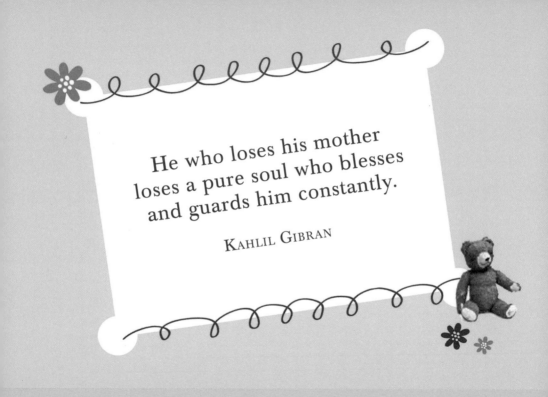

He who loses his mother
loses a pure soul who blesses
and guards him constantly.

KAHLIL GIBRAN

A baby fills a place in your heart that you never knew was empty.

UNKNOWN

A mother's heart is a baby's most beautiful dwelling.

ED DUSSAULT

My mother's love is the Almond Blossom of my mind, and the fragrance is worth dying for. Her gentle, compassionate touch shaped my very essence, and I will always attempt to become the man that she perceived me to be.

Frank L. de Roos III

Parenthood is a partnership with God.
You are working with the Creator
of the universe in shaping human character
and determining destiny.

RUTH VAUGHN

*Like kites without strings
and butterfly wings, my mother
taught me to soar with my dreams.*

WILLIAM H. MCMURRAY III

To be a mother is a woman's greatest vocation in life. She is a partner with God.

Spencer W. Kimball

The noblest calling in the world is that of a mother.

DAVID O. MCKAY

Everybody knows that a
good mother gives her children
a feeling of trust and stability.
She is the one they can count on
for the things that matter
most of all.

KATHARINE BUTLER HATHAWAY

A mother is God's deputy on earth!

RACHEL L. VARNHAGEN

There is no friendship, no love,
like that of the mother for the child.

HENRY WARD BEECHER

The power of one mother's prayers could stand an army on its ear.

ELIZABETH DEHAVEN

A woman that feareth the LORD,
she shall be praised.

PROVERBS 31:30 KJV

Mother: The person who sits up with you when you are sick and puts up with you when you are well.

UNKNOWN

The imprint of the mother
remains forever
on the life
of the child.

UNKNOWN

To a child's ear,
"mother" is magic
in any language.

ARLENE BENEDICT

A happy family is but an earlier heaven.

JOHN BOWRING

A child needs a mother more than all the things money can buy.

Ezra Benson

Love each other as God loves you, with an intense and particular love.

MOTHER TERESA

Her dignity consists in being unknown to the world; her glory is in the esteem of her husband; her pleasures in the happiness of her family.

JEAN-JACQUES RUSSEAU

The great academy,
a mother's knee.

THOMAS CARLYLE

Only mothers can think
of the future, because
they give birth to it
in their children.

MAXIM GORKY

Mother's love is peace.
It need not be acquired,
it need not be deserved.

ERICH FROMM

Some people come into
our lives and quickly go.
Some stay awhile and leave footprints
on our hearts, and we are never, ever, the same.

FLAVIA WEEDN

There is no love like a mother's
love, no stronger bond on earth. . .
like the precious bond that
comes from God to a mother,
when she gives birth.

JILL LEMMING

Your greatest pleasure is that which rebounds from hearts that you have made glad.

HENRY WARD BEECHER

*Mother: the most
beautiful word
on the lips
of mankind.*

KAHLIL GIBRAN

I will lie down and sleep,
for you alone,
OLᴏʀᴅ, make me dwell in safety.

Psᴀʟᴍ 4:8 ɴɪᴠ

My mother. . .taught me about the power of inspiration and courage, and she did it with a strength and a passion that I wish could be bottled.

CARLY FIORINA

The remembrance of a beloved mother becomes a shadow to all our actions; it precedes or follows them.

UNKNOWN

Is my mother my friend?
First of all she is my mother;
she's something sacred to me.
I love her dearly. . .yes, she is
also a good friend, someone
I can talk openly with if I want to.

JAMES RUSSELL LOWELL

The consciousness of children is formed by the influences that surround them; their notions of good and evil are the result of the moral atmosphere they breathe.

JEAN PAUL RICHTER

The mother loves her child
most divinely, not when
she surrounds him with comfort
and anticipates his wants,
but when she resolutely holds him
to the highest standards and
is content with nothing
less than his best.

HAMILTON WRIGHT MABIE

God, grant me courage
and hope for every day,
Faith to guide me along the way,
Understanding and wisdom, too,
And grace to accept what
life gives me to do.

HELEN STEINER RICE

My mom taught me to be
the best person you can be.
Strive to live your life to the fullest,
and don't let one day go by
without trying to live it
the best way you can.

UNKNOWN

A mother's love is unconditional and will touch a child's heart for years to come.

WANDA E. BRUNSTETTER

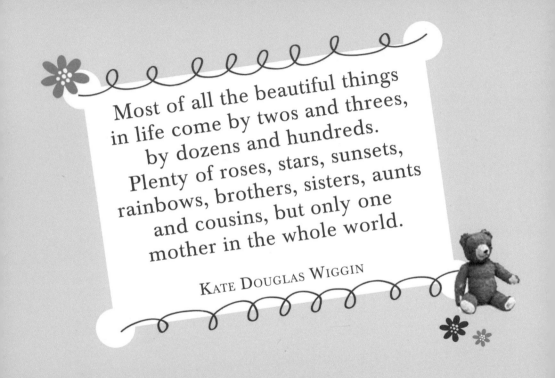

Most of all the beautiful things
in life come by twos and threes,
by dozens and hundreds.
Plenty of roses, stars, sunsets,
rainbows, brothers, sisters, aunts
and cousins, but only one
mother in the whole world.

KATE DOUGLAS WIGGIN

You should clothe yourselves instead with the beauty that comes from within, the unfading beauty of a gentle and quiet spirit, which is so precious to God.

1 PETER 3:4 NLT